# especially

## Moms

### by robert j. strand

## ORDERING INFORMATION

Individual sales can be had at selected bookstores or you can order direct from Rojon, Inc. at P. O. Box 3898, Springfield, MO 65808-3898 or call our customer service number, 1-888-389-0225.

Quantity sales are available at special discounts, bulk purchases or case lots by corporations, associations, churches and others. For details, contact Rojon, Inc. at the above address.

Orders by trade bookstores and wholesalers can be made through the above address as well.

ISBN: 0-9717039-2-2

Second Printing: January 2006

All Scripture references are from The New King James Version (Thomas Nelson Publishers) unless otherwise noted.

You can also make contact at the above address for speaking engagements, writers' seminars, keynote addresses or other books by the writer, Robert J. Strand.

**ROJON PUBLISHING**
P.O. Box 3898
Springfield, MO 65808-3898

Design and layout by Marc McBride

Presented to: _____

Presented by: _____

Date: _____

# DEDICATION:

*To all the mothers who are involved in the world's most exciting and yet unappreciated task of raising responsible citizens to become productive in today's world.*

*Further, as you give maternal love, a miraculous substance which God multiplies as He divides it, know that your sacrifices live on in the next generations.*

*BLESSINGS*

# CONTENTS

# THE DAFFODIL PRINCIPLE

**Several times my daughter had phoned to say,** "Mother, you must come see the daffodils before they are over." I wanted to go, but it was a two hour drive from Laguna to Lake Arrowhead.

"I will come next Tuesday," I promised, reluctantly on her third call.

Next Tuesday dawned cold and rainy. Still, a promise is a promise and so I drove it. At Carolyn's home I hugged and greeted the grandchildren and said, "Forget the daffodils, Carolyn! The road is invisible in the clouds and the fog and rain. There is nothing in the world except you and these grandkids that I want to see bad enough to make this drive."

My daughter smiled and said, "We drive in this all the time, Mother."

"Well, you won't get me back on the road until it clears and then I'm heading for home!" I assured her.

"I was hoping you'd take me over to the garage to pick up my car."

"How far do we have to drive?"

"Just a few blocks," Carolyn replied. "I'll drive. I'm used to this."

We all piled into the car and after some minutes I asked, "Where are we going? This isn't the way to the garage!"

"We're taking the long way," Carolyn smiled, "by way of the daffodils."

"Please turn around."

"It's all right, Mother, I promise. You will never forgive yourself if you miss this experience."

After another fifteen minutes, we turned onto a gravel road and I saw a small white church. On the far side of the church, I saw a hand-lettered sign: "Daffodil Garden." We got out of the car and each took a child's hand and walked down the path. Then, we turned a corner and I looked and gasped...

Before us lay the most glorious sight! It looked as though someone had taken a vat of gold and poured it down over the mountain peak and slopes. The flowers were planted in majestic, swirling patterns and ribbons and swaths of orange, white, lemon yellow, salmon pink, saffron and butter yellow. It was more than five acres of incredible beauty.

"Who has done this?" I asked Carolyn.

"It's just one woman," she answered. "She lives over there. That's her home," as she pointed to a well kept, modest, frame house.

We walked to the house. On the patio we saw a poster: "ANSWERS TO THE QUESTIONS I KNOW YOU ARE ASKING" was the headline. The first answer read: "50,000 bulbs." The second answer was: "One at a time, by one woman. Two hands, two feet, and very little brain." The third answer was: "Began in 1958."

There it is: "THE DAFFODIL PRINCIPLE!"

## What's the 'Daffodil Principle'?

You can change your world, one bulb at a time, one day at a time, one woman at a time, to bring your vision of beauty and joy to your world and the world your children will be living in!

*Then He said to them all, "If anyone desires to come after Me, let them deny themselves and take up their cross daily, and follow Me."*
*(Luke 9:23)*

# IT WILL TAKE A MIRACLE

**Tess went to her bedroom** and pulled a glass jelly jar from its hiding place in the closet. She poured all the change out on the floor and counted it carefully… three times, even. The total had to be just right. No chance for a mistake here. Carefully putting the coins back in the jar and twisting on the cap, she slipped out the back door and made her way six blocks to Rexall's Drug Store with the big red Indian Chief sign above the door. She waited patiently for the pharmacist to give her some attention but he was busy.

Tess twisted her feet to make a scuffling noise. Nothing. She cleared her throat. No good. Finally she took a quarter from the jar and banged it on the glass counter. That did it!

"And what do you want?" the pharmacist asked in an annoyed tone of voice. "I'm talking to my brother who is visiting from Chicago whom I haven't seen in ages," he said without waiting for a reply to his question.

"Well, I want to talk to you about my brother," Tess answered back in her annoyed tone of voice. "He's really, really sick… and I want to buy a miracle."

"I beg your pardon?" said the pharmacist.

"His name is Andrew and he has something bad growing inside his head and my Daddy says only a miracle can save him now. So how much does a miracle cost?"

"We don't sell miracles here, little girl. I'm sorry but I can't help you," the pharmacist replied, softening his tone of voice a little.

"Listen, I have the money to pay for it. If it isn't enough, I will get the rest. Just tell me how much it costs."

The pharmacist's brother had been listening to this conversation. He stooped down and asked the little girl, "What kind of a miracle does your brother need?"

"I don't know," Tess replied with tears welling up in her eyes. "I just know he's really,

really sick and Mommy says he needs an operation. But my Daddy can't pay for it, so I want to use my money."

"How much do you have?" asked the man from Chicago.

"One dollar and eleven cents," Tess answered, barely audible. "It's all the money I have."

"Well, what a coincidence," smiled the man. "A dollar and eleven cents is the exact price of a miracle for little brothers."

He took her glass jelly jar in one hand; with the other he grasped her little hand inside of the mitten and said, "Take me to where you live. I want to see your little brother and meet your parents. Let's see if I have the kind of a miracle you need."

The brother from Chicago was Dr. Carlton Armstrong, a surgeon, specializing in neuro-surgery. The operation was completed without charge and it wasn't long until Andrew was home again and doing well. Mom and Dad were happily talking about the chain of events that had led them to this moment. "That surgery," her mother whispered, "was a real miracle. I wonder how much it would have cost?"

Tess smiled. She knew exactly how much a miracle cost... one dollar and eleven cents... plus the faith of a little girl.

## What is a Miracle?

A miracle is not the suspension of natural law, but the operation of a higher law!

*Now God worked unusual miracles by the hands of Paul. (Acts 19:11)*

# WHY MOTHERS HAVE GRAY HAIR

**The CEO of a Fortune 500 company** needed to call one of his management employees about an urgent problem with one of their main computers. He dialed the employee's cell phone number and was greeted with a child's whispered "Hello."

Feeling a bit put out at the inconvenience of having to talk to a youngster the boss asked, "Is your Daddy home?"

"Yes," whispered the small voice.

"May I talk with him?" the man asked.

To the surprise of the CEO, the small voice whispered, "No."

Wanting to talk to an adult, the boss asked, "Is your Mommy there?"

"Yes," came the whispered answer.

"May I talk with her?"

"No," came the little voice.

Knowing that it was not likely that a young child would be left home alone, the CEO decided he would just leave a message with the person who should be present watching over this child.

"Is there any one there besides you?" he asked.

"Yes," whispered the child, "a policeman."

Wondering what a cop would be doing at his employee's home and now a bit alarmed, the boss asked, "May I speak with the policeman?"

"No, he's busy," whispered the child.

"Busy doing what?" asked the CEO.

"Talking to Daddy and Mommy and the fireman," came another whispered answer.

Growing even more concerned, he heard what sounded like a helicopter through the phone. So he asked, really alarmed, "What is that noise?"

"A hello-copper," answered the whispering voice.

"What is going on there?" asked the boss, more alarmed.

"The search team just landed the hello-copper," came back the awed whisper.

Alarmed, concerned, worried and more than just a little frustrated, the boss asked, "What are they searching for?"

Still whispering, the young voice replied, along with a muffled giggle: "Me!"

## What is a Sense of Humor?

"Humor has always been an expression of the freedom of the human spirit. It is an ability to stand outside of life's flow and view the whole scene... the incongruities, the tragedies outside our control, the unexpected."

*Dr. Terry L. Paulson*

*A merry heart does good like medicine,*
*But a broken spirit dries the bones.*
*(Proverbs 17:22)*

# TEACHING JOY IN WORK

**Lucy Calkins writes:** I used to believe I was doing my kids a favor when I pretended that I didn't want to spend a morning writing in my attic office or working at Teachers College. I'd say, "I'd rather be home with you. But I have no choice; I have to go to work."

Then I heard my sons begin to moan when it was time for them to do their schoolwork, and I realized what I'd done. If I had been honest, I would have told them that few things delight me more than the chance to spend a morning at my desk, and that I head off to Teachers College feeling as if I'm on my way to a clubhouse filled with friends. Now my sons know this, and they know I wish for them to approach their work with equal delight.

My youngest adores school, and I take advantage of this: "Who loves school?" I say, "You get a chance to work alongside your friends; what a treat!"

Miles loves school, too, but he sometimes sounds as if he has mixed feelings about it, so I make it a point to seem perplexed when he complains about having to go to school. "I can't imagine why you don't love it," I say. "I mean, would you rather spend the day hanging around doing nothing? That'd be so dull!"

*Lucy Calkins with Lydia Bellino, Raising Lifelong Learners,*
*Pereus Books, Reading Massachusetts, 1997*

## Parents Improve Performance

"Parents are their children's first teachers, and they serve as role models for peaceful living throughout the school years. Children whose parents are involved in their education achieve more than children whose parents are not involved."

*Dr. Vicki Mather of the Alberta Teacher's Association*

*My son, hear the instruction of your father,*
*And do not forsake the law of your mother:*
*For they will be a graceful ornament on your head,*
*And chains about your neck.*
*(Proverbs 1:8-9)*

When sharing blessings, acceptance or praise... it doesn't necessarily have to be a special occasion. Do it and do it often. Let these things become important in your thinking and vocabulary. Give it as a response even when a child least expects it. Too many children go through life seeking for approval... don't withhold it when it is in your power to speak it! Here they are:

WOW... Way to go... Super... You're special... Outstanding... Excellent... Great... Good... Neat... Well done... Remarkable... I knew you could do it... I'm proud of you... Fantastic... Super star... Nice work... Looking good... You're on top of it... Beautiful... Now you're flying... You're catching on... Now you've got it... You're incredible... Bravo... You're fantastic... Hurray for you... You're on target... You're on your way... How nice... How smart... Good job... That's incredible... Hot dog... Dynamite... You're beautiful... You're unique... Nothing can stop you now... Good for you... I like you... You're a winner... Remarkable job... Beautiful work... Spectacular ... You're spectacular... You're darling... You're precious... Great discovery... You've discovered the secret... You figured it out... Fantastic job... Hip, hip, hurray... Bingo... Magnificent... Marvelous... Terrific... You're important... Phenomenal...You're sensational... Super work... Creative work... Super job... Fantastic job... Exceptional performance... You're a real trooper... You are responsible... You are exciting... You learned it right... What an imagination... What a good listener... You are fun... You're growing up... You tried hard... You care... Beautiful sharing... Outstanding performance... You're a good friend... I trust you... You're important... You mean a lot to me... You make me happy... You belong... You've got a friend ... You make me laugh... You brighten my day... I respect you... You mean the world to me... That's correct... You're a joy... You're a treasure... You're wonderful...

You're perfect... Awesome... A+ job... You're a-okay... My buddy... You made my day... That's the best... A big hug... A big kiss...
I LOVE YOU!! *Compliments, Charter Hospital of Sioux Falls, South Dakota*

And always remember: A smile is an unspoken blessing that is worth a thousand words! It's even more powerful when you combine a smile with a word of encouragement, a word of praise, or a word of blessing.

## Just Do It!!

Mom, you no longer have an excuse because you can't find the right words at the right moment. Perhaps you are thinking: "My parents never blessed me with these kinds of words in this way." Or... it's possible that you may have been a victim of neglect and because of it you are making your own children victims of your neglect and hurt. I challenge you to break this cycle of silence! Begin today sharing acceptance and blessing! And one more word. No, you can't do it too much, if you are consistent so your children know it is meaningful and comes honestly.

**Just do it!**

You, too, will be blessed and will have become a blessing!

*This is the way you shall bless the children...Say to them: "The LORD bless you and keep you; The LORD make His face shine upon you, And be gracious to you; The LORD lift up His countenance upon you, And give you peace. (Numbers 6:23b-26)*

# RADICAL PARENTING

Jesse Jackson has a new and revolutionary program. This program would shake America to its far extremes. It would change life as we know it. It is extreme. These would work if they were instituted and practiced in all of our homes. Here they are:

**FIRST PRINCIPLE:** Parents should always take their children to school.
**SECOND PRINCIPLE:** Parents should meet their children's teachers.
**THIRD PRINCIPLE:** Parents and teachers should exchange telephone numbers.
**FOURTH PRINCIPLE:** Parents should pick up their children's report cards.
**FIFTH PRINCIPLE:** This is the really revolutionary one...parents should turn the television off for three hours every evening.

*David Shribman, Boston Globe*

In general, Western society has... by rushing children and forcing them through standardized curricula... virtually destroyed their creative potential. Children need time to think... undisturbed and uncurbed by fixed subject lines. When you do ask questions, be patient and give them time to answer! The average ineffective teacher waits only a split second for an answer. Effective teachers wait at least four times as long. Great teachers often ask why and how questions for which they are willing to wait for answers as long as a year!

*Raymond & Dorothy Moore,*
*Home Style Teaching, Word Publishing, Dallas, TX, p. 90*

# TWO SETS OF SCARS

**It happened on a hot summer day in south Florida** when a small boy decided to go for a swim in the old swimming hole behind his house. In a hurry to dive into the cool water, he ran out the back door leaving behind shoes, socks and shirt as he went. He dived into the water, not realizing that as he swam out toward the middle of the lake, an alligator was swimming toward shore!

His mother, in the house, looked out the window and saw the two as they got closer and closer together. In utter fear, she ran toward the water, screaming to her son as loudly as she could, about the danger. Hearing her voice, he, too, became alarmed and made a quick u-turn to swim back to shore. It was too late! She ran out on the dock to help him. But just as he reached her, the alligator caught up to him! From the dock, the mother grabbed her son by the arms just as the alligator bit down on his legs.

That began an incredible tug-of-war between the two. The alligator was much stronger than the mother... but the mother was much too passionate and adrenaline-pumped to let go!

A farmer neighbor happened to drive by. Hearing her screams he grabbed his gun, raced from his truck, took aim and shot the alligator, rescuing the boy!

Remarkably, after weeks in the hospital, this little guy survived. His legs were scarred from the vicious attack of the animal and on his arms were deep scratches where his mother's fingernails had dug into his flesh in her effort to hang on to the son she loved.

A newspaper reporter interviewed the boy after the trauma and asked him to show his scars. The boy lifted his pant legs. And then, with obvious pride, he said to the reporter, "But look at my arms. I have scars on my arms, too. I have them because my mom wouldn't let go!"

## What About Your Scars?

Perhaps we can identify with that boy. We have scars, too. Maybe not from an alligator or anything quite so dramatic, but, maybe scars from a painful past.

Some may have caused regrets. But some wounds, mother, are because God refused to let go. In the middle of your struggle, He's been there holding on to you, all the time.

If you have the scars of His love on your arms... be very grateful He did not let go and in the future He will not let go!

*For He Himself has said, "I will never leave you nor forsake you." So we may boldly say:*
*"The Lord is my helper;*
*I will not fear. What can man do to me?"*
*(Hebrews 13:5b-6)*

# GOD DANCES ON POTATO CHIPS

**Not too long ago, I had "one-of-those-days."** The children had been acting up! There was pressure from a writing deadline! Company was to arrive in a couple of days and the toilet was plugged. I went to the bank and the trainee had to do my deposit three times and then called for help. At the supermarket the lines stretched forever. Traffic was horrendous! By the time I got home I was frazzled, sweaty and in a hurry to get something on the table for dinner.

Deciding on "Campbell's" cream of mushroom soup, I grabbed a can opener, cranked open the can and remembered I had forgotten to buy milk. Skip the soup idea. On to "plan B" which was left-over baked beans. I took the "Tupperware" container from the fridge and popped the seal, took one look and groaned. My husband isn't a picky eater but even HE won't eat baked beans that look like dried up caterpillars. Really frustrated now, I decided on a menu that is as fool proof as it is nutrition-free: hot dogs and potato chips!

Retrieving a brand new bag of chips from the cupboard, I grasped the cellophane and gave a hearty pull. It didn't open! I tried again. Nothing happened. I took a deep breath, doubled my muscle and yanked! With a loud pop, the cellophane gave way, all the way, ripping from top to bottom! Chips flew everywhere! It was the economy size, too! It was the final straw. I let out a blood curdling scream: "I CAN'T TAKE IT ANYMORE!"

My husband heard my cry of frustration. Within seconds he was standing in the doorway, surveying the damage… an opened can of soup, melting groceries, moldy baked beans, hot dogs on the cupboard and one frustrated, quivering wife standing ankle deep in potato chips!

He did the most helpful thing he could think of at this moment. He took a flying jump, landing flat-footed in the pile of chips! He began to stomp and dance and twirl, grinding those chips into my tile floor in the process!

I stared, I fumed, I screamed! Pretty soon I was working to stifle a smile... it was a sight to behold! Eventually I had to laugh! And finally, I decided to join him. I too, took a jump onto the chips... and then, I danced, too! Now, I'll be the first to admit my husband's response wasn't the one I was looking for. But the truth is... it was exactly what I needed!

I didn't need a clean up crew or a personal chef as much as I needed an ATTITUDE ADJUSTMENT! The kids came running to see what the excitement was all about and joined in the laughter. And the laughter from that rather funky moment provided the adjustment needed!

*The Source shall remain anonymous, as the memory is too painful to this day.*

## Has God Ever Stomped On Your Chips?

I know that in my life, there have been plenty of times when I've gotten myself into frustrating situations and have cried for help. All the time I prayed and hoped that God would show up with a celestial broom and clean up the mess I've made of things. What often happens instead is that God dances on my chips, answering my prayer in a completely different way than I had expected, but in a way that is best for me after all!

*Call upon Me in the day of trouble;*
*I will deliver you, and you shall glorify Me.*
*(Psalm 50:15)*

# WHAT'S FIRST IN THE FAMILY?

**Tony Evans writes,** a point was driven home to me during my high school football days, when I would often drag my weary body home after practice and stumble through the door. With a loud yawn, I'd say, "Mom, I'm tired. I'm going up to rest."

Before I made it up three steps, my mother would call back, "Son, you better come down here and get your chores done first."

"But I'm tired!" I'd protest.

"Wrong answer!" Mom replied. "If tiredness was a criteria of function you would not have any clothes washed or dinner cooked. In fact, I would have gotten rid of you the day after you were born!"

I got the message. Mom was reminding me that as part of a family, I had obligations and responsibilities that didn't evaporate simply because I didn't feel like fulfilling them.

*Tony Evans, The Importance of Church Membership, a booklet*

There are lots of benefits associated with being part of a family… and rightfully so. However, at the same time, in order to keep this kind of support from running out, each member is required to do his or her share. It's the continued investment of the time and resources of each family member that makes it happen. And there is not a home around that can function without this important kind of support.

We are building homes better so that we can have a better church so that together we can build a better society so that we can make the world a better place in which we can all function as family.

## God Works Through Us

"The ideal is not that we do work for God,
but that we are so loyal to Him that He can do His work
through us...
"I reckon on you for extreme service,
with no complaining on your part and no explanation on Mine."
God wants to use us as He used His own Son."

*Oswald Chambers*

*For as we have many members in one body, but all the members
do not have the same function,
so we being many, are one body in Christ,
and individually members of one another.
(Romans 12:4-5)*

We were sittin' 'round our table just a talkin' 'bout
   Our Lord.
I said "What did Jesus look like Mom? I can't find
   it in the Word."
I said "I read about our Savior in the Good Book
   as you know,
But the Bible just don't tell me things that I'd like
   to know."
I said, "The Bible will not tell me the color of His
   eyes,
His special style of clothing, nor even what's His
   size."
"Did He wear His hair cut short, or did He let it
   grow?"
"Mom, why don't this Bible tell me things that I
   would like to know?"

Mom put an arm around me and said, "Son, let's
   take a look."
Then with her gentle, work-scarred hands, she
   opened up the Book.
Oh, she bowed her head and said a prayer, but
   Momma did that every time.
Then she started flippin' through the pages and
   said, "Let's see what we can find."
She said, "Doesn't He look gentle here as He
   holds this little child?"
And "Oh, there's the man side of Him, son, in the
   Temple gone half wild."
She said, "We can see His great compassion as
   He heals the leper's sores."

And "He has mercy on the prostitute, bound for
    Hell's dark shores."
She said, "My, He looks so humble as He washes
    all their feet."
"Imagine the power that divides five loaves and
    fishes, so several thousand souls might eat."
She said, "Son, you forget about His hair and
    clothes and the color of His eyes."
"It's not an accident, my child, that we're not told
    His size."
"For those are only outside things, they'd just get
    in the way..." like color, clothes, and those
    outside things do so much today."
She said, "No, my son, we'll never know how
    many tears He cried."
"And we can never feel the agony He must have
    felt inside."
"But we can see Him clearly there as He hangs
    on Calvary's tree."
"And we can tell the world about the awesome
    love He has for you and me."

Well, my Momma's gone, but the Book's still
    there, it's pages worn and read. Now every
    time I pick it up, I hear what Momma said.
Friends we can see what Jesus looked like, if we
    will only look.
We just need to look inside, MY MOMMA'S
    PICTURE BOOK!

*Author is unknown*

# THE HOSTILE WITNESS

**A small town prosecutor called his first witness to the stand** in what promised to be a spectacular trial. She was an elderly woman who presented herself as a mother of four and grandmother of nine. After she was sworn in, the lawyer approached her and asked, "Ma'am, do you know who I am?"

She answered, "Oh, yes, I do know you. I've known you since you were a little boy. And honestly… you've been a considerable disappointment. You lie, you cheat, you manipulate and you talk about people behind their backs. You think that you are a real big shot, but you are just a loud-mouthed brat who does not have the brains of a cocker spaniel. Oh yes, I know you."

The prosecutor was stunned and wasn't sure what to say next. In a panic, the prosecutor pointed across the room and inquired, "Ma'am, do you know the defense attorney?"

She again answered, "I most certainly do, young man. I've known him even longer than I've known you. I baby-sat for him on many occasions. He, too, has been a bitter disappointment to me. He's lazy, cruel and he has a drinking problem. The man has never had a normal relationship with anyone. He has one of the sleaziest law practices in this entire state. And besides that he has cheated on his wife with at least three different women. I most certainly do know him."

At this point the judge banged his gavel and called the two lawyers up to the bench. The judge carefully and forcefully instructed them by saying, "If either of you asks that woman if she knows me, I'm going to charge you with contempt of court and throw out your case!"

## The Surly Bird
Research has shown that cheerful people are more resistant to disease than miserable folk.
In other words, it's the surly bird that catches the germ.

## THEN, There are Quiet Friends
"I'm finding that saying less is better. Talking too quickly, too much, and too cutely is destructive to the spirit.
The spiritual men and women I've come to admire were generally quiet-spirited and more silent than verbose."

*Gordon MacDonald*

*Even so the tongue is a little member and boasts great things.*
*See how great a forest fire a little fire kindles!*
*(James 3:5)*

**Several years ago,** a poverty stricken boy was selling trinkets from door-to-door in order to pay his way through school. On one particular day he found himself down to his last thin dime and he was hungry.

He decided he would ask for a meal at the next house. However, he lost his nerve when a beautiful young woman opened the door. Instead of asking for a meal, he asked for a drink of water.

She thought he looked sort of hungry so she brought him a large glass of milk and some cookies instead. He drank it slowly and then asked, "How much do I owe you?"

"You don't owe me anything," she replied. "Mother has taught us never to accept pay for a kindness."

"Then I thank you from the bottom of my heart," he replied. As Howard Kelly left that house, he not only felt stronger physically but his faith in God and human beings was strengthened. He had been ready to give up and quit.

Many years later that same young woman became critically ill. The local doctors were baffled by her condition. She was finally sent to the big city where they called in specialists to study her rare disease. Dr. Howard Kelly was called for the consultation.

When he heard the name of the town she came from, a strange light filled his eyes. Immediately he went down the hall of the hospital to her room. Dressed in his physicians gown he went in to see her. He recognized her instantly. He went back to the consultation room determined to do his best to save her life. He gave special attention to her case. After a long struggle, the battle was won… he had saved her life.

Dr. Kelly requested the business office to give him the final bill for approval. He looked at it and wrote something on the bottom of the bill before it was sent to her room.

She was afraid to open it because she was sure it might take all her resources to pay for it. Finally, she looked and on the bottom she read these words:

*"Paid in full with one cold glass of milk and some cookies."*

*Dr. Howard Kelly.*

Tears of joy flooded her eyes as her happy heart gave praise and thanks: "Thank you, God, that Your love has also been shared through another human being because of the lessons shared with me by my mother."

## Friends With God

"It is a staggering thing, but it is true...the relationship in which sinful human beings know God is one in which God, so to speak, takes them on His staff, to be henceforth His fellow workers and personal friends."

*J. I. Packer*

*No longer do I call you servants, for a servant does not know what his master is doing: but I have called you friends, for all things that I heard from My Father I have made known to you. You did not choose Me, but I chose you and appointed you that you should go and bear fruit, and that your fruit should remain, that whatever you ask the Father in My name He may give you. (John 15:15-16)*

# THE BIRTH OF A SONG

**He writes in his own words:** Back in 1932, I was 32 years old and a new husband. My wife, Nettie, and I were living in a little apartment on Chicago's Southside. One hot August afternoon I had to go to St. Louis, where I was to be the featured soloist at a large revival meeting. I didn't want to go. Nettie was in the last month of pregnancy with our first child. But a lot of people were expecting me in St. Louis. I kissed Nettie good-bye, clattered downstairs to our Model A and, in a fresh Lake Michigan breeze, chugged out of Chicago on Route 66.

However, outside the city, I discovered that in my anxiety at leaving, I had forgotten my music case. I wheeled around and headed back. I found Nettie sleeping peacefully. I hesitated at her bed; something was strongly telling me to stay. But eager to get on my way and not wanting to disturb Nettie, I shrugged off the feeling and quietly slipped out of the room with my music.

The next night in the steaming St. Louis heat, the crowd called on me to sing again and again. When I finally sat down, a messenger boy ran up with a Western Union telegram. I ripped open the envelope. Pasted on the yellow sheet were the words: YOUR WIFE JUST DIED.

People were happily singing and clapping around me, but I could not keep from crying. I rushed to a phone and called home. All I could hear on the other end was, "Nettie is dead. Nettie is dead."

When I got back to Chicago, I learned that Nettie had given birth to a boy. I swung between grief and joy. Yet that night, the baby died. I buried Nettie and our little boy together in the same casket. Then I fell apart. For days I closeted myself. I felt that God had done me an injustice. I didn't want to serve Him anymore or write Gospel songs. I just wanted to go back to that jazz world I once knew so well.

But then, as I hunched alone in that dark apartment those first sad days, I thought back to the afternoon I went to St. Louis. Something kept telling me to stay with Nettie. Was that something God? Oh, if I had paid more attention to Him that day. From that moment on I vowed to listen more closely to Him. But still I was lost in grief. Everyone was kind to me, especially a friend,

Professor Fry, who seemed to know what I needed.

On the following Saturday evening he took me up to Malone's Poro College, a neighborhood music school. I sat down at the piano and my hands began to browse over the keys. Something happened to me then. I felt at peace. I felt as though I could reach out and touch God. I found myself playing a melody:

*Precious Lord, take my hand, lead me on,*
*Let me stand!*
*I am tired, I am weak, I am worn,*
*Through the storm, through the night,*
*Lead me on to the light.*
*Take my hand, precious Lord,*
*Lead me home!*

As the Lord gave me these words and melody, He also healed my spirit. I learned that when we are in our deepest grief, when we feel farthest from God, this is when He is closest and when we are most open to His restoring power. And so I go on living for God willingly and joyfully, until that day comes when He will take me and gently lead me home.

Who is this song writer? Tommy Dorsey!

*Fear not, for I have redeemed you: I have called you by your name;*
*You are mine, When you pass through the waters, I will be with you;*
*And through the rivers, they shall not overflow you. When you walk*
*through the fire, you shall not be burned, Nor shall the flame scorch you.*
*For I am the LORD your God! (Isaiah 43:1b-3a)*

# THOUGHTS FROM A WOMAN'S WORLD

Laugh and the world laughs with you. Cry and you cry with your girlfriends.
*Laurie Kuslansky*

My second favorite household chore is ironing. My first being, hitting my head on the top bunk until I faint.
*Erma Bombeck*

The phrase "working mother" is redundant.
*Jane Sellman*

Whatever women must do they must do twice as well as men to be thought half as good. Luckily, this is not difficult.
*Charlotte Whitton, Mayor of Ottawa*

In politics, if you want anything said, ask a man... if you want anything done, ask a woman.
*Margaret Thatcher*

A man's got to do what a man's got to do. A woman must do what he can't.
*Rhonda Hansome*

Many women are more than able to take a good joke. Many husbands are living proof.
*Donna M. Strand*

Women have many faults. Men only two: everything they say and everything they do.
*Elizabeth Hodgin*

Don't be so humble. You're not that great.
*Golda Meir*

Few women admit their age. Few men act theirs.
*An anonymous female*

Marriage is a great institution, but I'm not ready for an institution just yet.
*Mae West*

# EXCHANGING OUR RICHES

**During his reign, King Frederick William III,** of Prussia found himself in deep trouble. The wars which had been fought had been very costly and in trying to rebuild the nation, found that he and the treasury were seriously short of finances. He couldn't disappoint his people and surrender to the enemy. That was not an option. What would he do? What could he do?

After careful thought and reflection, he decided to appeal to the women of Prussia. He humbly asked them to bring their jewelry of gold, diamonds, precious stones and silver. He would have the precious stones taken out of their settings and sold. The gold and silver would be melted for the sake of their country. For each piece of jewelry received, he determined to exchange a decoration or medal of bronze or iron as a symbol of his gratitude. Each decoration would be inscribed: "I GAVE GOLD FOR IRON, 1813."

The response was overwhelming! The wonderful women prized their gifts from the king more than their former jewelry. The reason why is clear, as we look back on this page of history: the decorations and medals were proof that they had sacrificed for their king! As a result, it also became unfashionable to wear any other kind of jewelry. Yes, more than enough money was raised to bring the country out of debt and begin the re-building process!

Incidentally, this event also established the "ORDER OF THE IRON CROSS."

I wondered as I wrote this... would the men of Prussia have been as willing to sacrifice as the women? I doubt it! In today's world I have observed that it's the women who are more willing to make sacrifices so that their family benefits!

Mother... let me be one of those to tell you: "THANK YOU FOR THE BIG AND LITTLE SACRIFICES YOU MAKE AS YOU BUILD YOUR HOME AND RAISE YOUR FAMILY!"

## Generosity or Reciprocity?

"As generosity becomes replaced by reciprocity, instead of reaching out to others in kindness for its own sake, we start to ask what we will receive for the assistance we are about to render.
Then, we stop giving freely of ourselves and we start keeping score or worse."

*Psychologist Aaron Hass*

*Give and it will be given to you:*
*good measure, pressed down, shaken together, and running over*
*will be put into your bosom.*
*For with the same measure that you use,*
*it will be measured back to you.*
*(Luke 6:38)*

There's something in a simple hug,
That always warms the heart,
It welcomes us back home,
and makes it easier to part.

A hug's a way to share the joy,
and sad times we go through,
or just a way for mothers to say,
they like you 'cause you're you.

Hugs are meant for anyone,
for whom we really care,
from your mother to your grandma to your neighbor,
or a cuddly bear.

A hug is an amazing thing,
it's just the perfect way,
to show the love we're feeling,
but can't find the words to say.

It's funny how a little hug,
makes everyone feel good,
in every place and language,
it's always understood.

And hugs don't need new equipment,
special batteries or parts,
just open up your arms,
and open up your hearts!

*Source is Unknown*

## Do It To Perfection

"Whenever things go a bit sour in a job I'm doing, I always tell myself, you can do better than this.
Why? Because I remembered my mother's words:
'Whatever you do, do it to perfection.'"

*Dr. Theodor Seuss*

*There is a friend who sticks closer than a brother.*
*(Proverbs 18:24b)*

# GOD MAKES CAKES

**A daughter, Susan, is telling her mother,** Evelyn, how everything is going wrong in her life… she's failing algebra, her boyfriend broke up with her, she failed her first driving test and now her very best friend is moving away!

Meanwhile, her mother continues preparing a cake for the oven and asks Susan if she would like a snack. Susan replied, "Absolutely, Mom, I love your cakes."

"Here, have some cooking oil," her mother offers.

"Yuck," says Susan.

"How about a couple of raw eggs?"

"Gross, Mom!"

"Would you like some flour, then? Or how about some baking soda?"

"Mom, those are all yucky!"

"Would you like to try some sugar?"

"That's not good for you."

To which Evelyn finally replies, "Yes, all those things seem bad all by themselves. But when they are put together in the right way, they make a wonderfully delicious cake!"

She paused for effect, looked Susan straight in the eyes and continued, "God works the same way. Many times we wonder why He would let us go through such bad and difficult times. But God knows that when He puts these things all in His order, they always work for our good. We just have to trust Him and, eventually, in His good timing, they will all make something wonderful!"

## Have You Ever Wondered?

What did I do to deserve this?
Why is this happening to me?
Doesn't God know that this is hurting me?
Well, we've just read a wonderful explanation!
That's still not enough of an explanation for you? Just read our verse for today, perhaps that's the explanation you really need and understand.

*Now He who searches the hearts knows what the mind of the Spirit is, because He makes intercession for the saints according to the will of God. And we know that all things work together for good to those who love God, to those who are the called according to His purpose!*
*(Romans 8:27-28)*

# THE MASTER PLAN

I formed a master plan for life
   In the green years' dawning glow,
Not comprehending, naively,
   The truth I could not know.

I only planned for happy hours,
   I sketched in sunny days;
On my horizon not a cloud
   Presaged the storm God's ways.

I left no place, no room at all,
   For grief; could not forsee
That pain and loss were down the way,
   Just waiting there for me.

I could not know my firstborn son
   Would have a stay so brief
And leave behind an emptiness
   Akin to a fallen leaf.

I hadn't left a space for loss,
   I only planned for gain,
But I expected rainbows
   Though unprepared for rain.

My plan was aimed for large success,
   No page contained defeat;
No slow, discouraged footsteps
   Trudged down my private street.

Then when life didn't follow through
   The blueprint I had made,
I couldn't understand at all
   And found myself dismayed.

But life wrote other plans for me,
   Which, wisely, it withheld
Until I learned I needed more
   Than what I'd blithely spelled.

And now in life's gray twilight,
   By pain and sorrow blessed,
I know how wisely life has planned:
   I know its plan was best.

*Gladys Lawler, age 93*

40

# THE VISION OF FUTURE GREATNESS

**When Luciono Pavarotti was a boy,** his grandmother put him on her lap and said, "You're going to be great, you'll see." And this she often repeated into his life... blessing him with a great vision of the future.

His mother hoped and dreamed of him becoming a banker.

"Instead," Pavarotti explains, "I ended up teaching elementary school and sang only infrequently. But my father constantly prodded me and said I was singing below my potential."

Finally, at the age of twenty-two, Pavarotti dumped teaching for selling life insurance to give him enough time and earnings in order to develop his vocal talent. He went to school, he took private lessons and practiced and practiced.

"Studying voice was the turning point of my life," says the world famous opera star. "It's a mistake to take the safe path in life. If I hadn't listened to my father and dropped teaching, I would never be here. And yes, my teacher groomed me. But no teacher ever told me I would become famous. Just my grandmother!"

The power of the spoken word into the life of a child can be life changing. When you think of it... the tongue holds the power of blessing or cursing, building up or tearing down, encouraging or discouraging. Mother, grandmother, stop and think with me... what kind of words have you been speaking into the ears of the children you love? When you bless with your words... you are giving approval, you are giving permission to succeed, you are raising the sights, you are creating a future vision, you are releasing that child to do and become all that they can be!

## Excellence

"None of us will ever accomplish anything excellent or commanding except when she listens to this whisper which is heard by her alone."

*Ralph Waldo Emerson*

*Do not withhold good from those to whom it is due,*
*When it is in the power of your hand to do so.*
*(Proverbs 3:27)*

**Pat Kerrigan is an American woman** who received her doctorate in psychology from the University of Michigan. She began her career as a public school teacher but then switched to a career in industry. She started in the area of human resources and went on from there.

She became the first and to this point, only woman, to manage a General Motors (GM) car assembly plant. How has she done in this male dominated business?

Under her leadership and management the plant received a "record corporate quality standard." What happened to achieve this high award? Here's the record: Grievances were reduced to zero after there had been record highs following a number of bitter strikes. Disciplinary incidents declined by 82% and productivity went up 40%!

How was this achieved? In a video that was made high-lighting her leadership style and ability, numerous supervisors and assembly line workers who operated under her management were interviewed. This was most interesting.

Their unanimous response was that she was the first plant manager to walk around and shake everybody's hand... from the lowest to the highest; from the janitors to the supervisors. She called them by name. She shared openly some of her personal experiences. She told stories. She asked about the workers and their families. She asked for their advice and input.

The bottom line consensus was that she became a real person... not just a person who holds an important position!

Is there a lesson here for all of us?

## Leadership is...
"A sacrifice...it is self-denial...it is love, it is fearlessness, it is humility, and it is in the perfectly disciplined will.
This is also the distinction between great and little people.
The harder you work, the harder it is to surrender.
The role of the leader is to enhance, transform, coach, care, trust, and cheerlead.
The activities of the leader are to educate, sponsor, coach, and counsel using appropriate timing, tone, consequences, and skills."
*Tom Peters and Nancy Austin, Passion for Excellence*

*The things which you have learned and received and heard and seen in me, these do, and the God of peace will be with you.*
*(Philippians 4:9)*

# BAD MOMMY!

**A young man was walking through a supermarket** to pick up a few items when he noticed an old lady following him around. Thinking nothing of it, he ignored her and continued on. Finally, he was ready to check out but she pushed her cart immediately in front of him in the line.

"Pardon me," she said sweetly, "I'm sorry if my staring at you has made you feel a bit uncomfortable. It's just that you look like my son, who died recently."

"I'm very sorry," replied the young man. "Is there anything I can do for you?"

"Yes," she said. "As I'm leaving after checking out, can you say 'Goodbye, Mother!'? It would really make me feel much better and make my day."

"Sure," replied the polite young man. As the old lady was leaving, with groceries in her cart, he called out, loudly, "Goodbye, Mother!"

Then, after he had unloaded his groceries and the checker was about to ring him up, he noticed that his total was already $137.47. "How can that be?" he asked, incredulous. "I only have just these few items."

"Your mother said that you would pay for her groceries," answered the clerk! Okay…

Even a bad example can be a learning experience. Humor happens when two worlds collide. Something unexpected has to happen that jolts you up and out of the normal life patterns and then you start laughing. Humor is the synapse between the ordinary and the surprising! Every time we laugh, we are making a leap between two worlds! And… in order to be the best mother possible… one ingredient is a well used sense of humor!

## The Use of Humor

"Humor used at the proper time can help break the "panic cycle" that so often accelerates a person's illness or state of mind. Laughter can broaden the focus and diffuse the intensity of negative thoughts, thereby aiding the person's ability to gain control."

*Norman Cousins*

"The kind of humor I like is the thing that makes me laugh for five seconds and think for ten minutes."

*William Davis*

"Though a humorist may bomb occasionally, it is still better to exchange humorists than bombs.
And... you can't fight when you're laughing."

*Jim Boren*

*To everything there is a season,*
*A time for every purpose under heaven:*
*A time to weep, And a time to laugh;*
*A time to mourn, and a time to dance!*
*(Ecclesiastes 3:1, 4)*

# THINGS LEARNED FROM CHILDREN

1. Garbage bags do not make good parachutes.
2. A three-year-old is louder than 200 adults in a crowded restaurant.
3. If you spray hair spray on dust bunnies and run over them with roller blades, they can ignite.
4. If you hook a dog leash over a ceiling fan, the motor is not strong enough to rotate a forty-two-pound boy wearing Batman underwear and a Superman cape. It is strong enough, however, to spread paint on all four walls of a large room.
5. When using the ceiling fan as a baseball bat, you have to throw the ball up a few times before you get a hit. A ceiling fan can hit a baseball a long way.
6. The glass in windows (even double or triple pane) doesn't stop a baseball hit by a ceiling fan.
7. When you hear the toilet flush and the words, "Uh-oh," at the same time, it's already too late.
8. Brake fluid mixed with Clorox makes smoke and lots of it.
9. A six-year-old can start a fire with a flint rock even though a thirty-six year old man says they can only do it in the movies. A magnifying glass can start a fire, even on an overcast day.
10. Certain sized "Legos" will eventually pass through the digestive tract of a four-year-old.
11. "Play-Doh" and "microwave" should never be used in the same sentence.
12. Super glue really is forever. And, yes, it does stick to fingers, tongues, ears, hair and toes as well as eyelids and eyebrows.

13. No matter how much Jell-O you put in a swimming pool, you still can't walk on water.
14. Pool filters do not like Jell-O.
15. VCRs do not eject PB&J (peanut butter and jelly) sandwiches even though TV commercials show that they do.
16. A king-sized waterbed holds enough water to fill a 2,000 square foot house to a depth of four inches.
17. Marbles in gas tanks make lots of noise in a moving car, van or SUV.
18. You probably do not want to know what that particular strange odor is.
19. Always look in the oven before you turn it on... as plastic toys do not like ovens very much. The same goes for microwaves or dishwashers or washing machines. Neither do vacuum cleaners like toys or coins or any other kind of trinket.
20. The spin cycle on the washing machine does make earth-worms dizzy. However, it also makes cats dizzy.
21. Cats will always spit up twice their body weight when dizzy or upset or when hung by their tails.
22. Anything whispered between parents can be heard loudly spoken to the town gossip in church the next Sunday.
23. Dogs and cats don't like each other when thrown together in the same kennel.
24. Mommies and Daddies are not happy when stepping on "Legos" at night in the dark.

# MOMMY SAY...

**When our daughter Laura was three-years-old,** she had a slight speech problem... enunciating her "Rs" and certain other sounds. At this time we were expecting our third child, Katie. If Katie happened to be a boy, we were naming him Joseph. Try as she might, Laura could not say Joseph. She pronounced it "Jofus." I remember trying to help her. I would get down on my knees, cup her little chin in my hands and look into her eyes. I would say, "Now, Laura, say 'Jo'."

And she would say, "Jo."

Then I would say, "Now, Laura, say 'Seph'."

And she would say, "Seph."

"Now, Laura, say 'Joseph'."

And she would say "Jofus." She just couldn't get it.

One summer day, shortly before Katie was born, I was out back playing whiffleball with Laura and her older brother, David, who was five. The big deal was to hit the ball over the fence for a homerun. David had done it... but Laura had never achieved this feat. Well... on this particular day she connected with one and hit it out for a homerun! She circled the yard and was very excited.

About then, her mother, Shelly, came out to the back yard and Laura yelled, "Mommy! Mommy! I hit a home run! I hit a homerun!" But Shelly couldn't understand her rapid fire speech and asked Laura to please repeat.

I'll never forget the scene... totally frustrated, Laura walked over to her mother, pulled her down to eye level, cupped Shelly's chin in her hands, looked into her eyes and said, "Mommy, say 'home....run'."

## A Small Girl's Essay on Parents

"The trouble with parents is they are so old when we get them,
it's hard to change their habits."

*Eleanor Doane*

*Train up a child*
*In the way s/he should go,*
*And when s/he is old*
*S/he will not depart from it.*
*(Proverbs 22:6)*

# A MOM'S LIFE

Take your plate into the kitchen.
Take it downstairs when you go.
Don't leave it there, take it upstairs.
Is that yours?
Don't hit your brother.
I'm talking to you.
Just a minute, please, can't you
      see I'm talking.
I said, Don't interrupt!
Did you brush your teeth?
Go back to bed.
You can't watch in the afternoon.
What do you mean, there's nothing to do?
Go outside.
Read a book.
Turn it down.
Get off the phone.
Tell your friend you'll call her back.
Right now!
Hello. No, she's not home.
She'll call you when she gets home.
Take a jacket. Take a sweater.
Take one anyway.
Someone left shoes in front of the TV.
Do you realize that could kill you?

Hurry up!
Hurry up!! Everyone's waiting.
I'll count to ten and then we leave
      without you.
Did you go to the bathroom?
If you don't go, you're not going.
Why didn't you go before you left?
Can you hold it?
What's going on back there?
Stop it.
I said, Stop it!
I don't want to hear about it.
Stop it or I'm taking you home right now.
That's it. We're going home.
Give me a kiss.
I need a hug.
Make your bed.
Clean up your room.
Set the table.
I need you to set the table!
Don't tell me it's not your turn.
Please move your chair in to the table.
Sit up.
Just try a little.
Get the toys out of the hall.

Get the boys out of the bathtub.
Get the toys off the stairs.
Is your homework done?
Stop yelling. If you want to ask me
    something, come here.
STOP YELLING. IF YOU WANT TO
    ASK ME SOMETHING,
    COME HERE.
I'll think about it.
Not now.
Ask your father.
We'll see.
Maybe sometime later.
Don't sit so close to the TV,
    it's bad for your eyes.
Calm down.
Calm down and start over.
Is that the truth?
Fasten your seat belt.
Did everyone fasten their seat belts?
I'm sorry, that's the rule.
I'm sorry, that's the rule.
Yes, I'm sorry, that is the rule!
I know it's silly, but that's the rule!
You don't have to eat the whole thing.

Stop playing and eat.
Would you watch what you are doing?
Move your glass. It's too close
    to the edge.
Watch it!
More, what?
More, please. That's better.
Just eat one bite of salad.
You don't always get what you want.
That's life. Don't argue with me.
I'm not discussing this any more.
Go to your room.
No, ten minutes are not up.
One more minute.
How many times have I told you,
    don't do that.
Where did the cookies go?
Eat the old fruit before you eat
    the new fruit.
Did you do what I asked you to do?
I'm sorry, that's the rule in this house.
Because I said so!
Because I'm the mother!

*Delia Ephron*

# BORN WITHOUT EARS

**A pastor received a frantic call from a new father.** This father explained that he wanted their pastor to be present when the mother came out from under the anesthetic and would be told she had given birth to a beautiful baby boy... healthy in every way, except the newborn had no ears!

When the pastor arrived, he joined the nervous first-time father and the doctor as they entered the room where the mother was recovering from an extremely difficult birth. The doctor explained that the baby had auditory openings and all the inner ear parts necessary to receive sounds but no fleshly part outside that we call the "ear." The doctor assured the parents that the problem could easily be corrected when the child's growth was completed and a matching donor was found.

School was a tough experience for this little guy. Many times he would come home crying, "I'm a freak! I'm nothing but a freak!" He was well aware of the stares, whispers, taunts and nicknames given to him by the other kids. Junior high was the worst of his growing up experiences but the young man began to adapt and live with his disfigurement. To cover it up he let his hair grow long and wore stocking caps. However, he also became an excellent student with plans to study geology.

One spring day, when he was a college sophomore, his father phoned with this news: "Well, Son, we've finally found an ear donor for you. The operation will take place this summer."

The operation was a rousing success. This young man was very happy as he returned to college in the fall. His new ears were beautiful and life took on new meanings for him. Even his social life with the girls improved.

He graduated with honors and, justifiably, his parents were proud of him as he left to take a job in the Midwest. Life was great. Then a call came from his father, "Son, your mother has had a heart attack. Please come right home, on the next flight."

He arrived as quickly as he could make arrangements, only to learn that his mother had passed away before his arrival. Two days later, at the funeral home, his father walked with him to the casket where she lay. They talked about what a wonderful mother she had been. As they stood together looking down at her… the father reached down and gently pushed back the mother's hair-do to reveal a well kept secret. His mother didn't have any ears. She had given them so he could become whole!

## Love
The love of God is greater even than this mother's love.
God gave us more than ears…
He gave His only Son!

*For God so loved the world that He gave His only begotten Son, that whosoever believeth in Him should not perish but have everlasting life!*
*(John 3:16)*

# FOR BETTER OR WORSE

**A man felt he deserved a long overdue pay raise.** He told his wife that he was going to ask his boss for one on this particular day. He promised that he wasn't going to leave the man's office until he had what was due him.

The opportunity to talk to the boss didn't happen as early in the day as he had planned. Toward the end of the day he finally raised his courage in order to approach his boss. To the man's surprise the employer readily agreed that he was due an increase in salary. In fact, the boss offered him more than he would have requested.

When the husband arrived home that evening he noticed the dining room was set for a lovely candlelight dinner for him and the family. The table was set with the best tablecloth, the best silverware, best china. She had prepared a festive, romantic, intimate dinner to celebrate. He thought that someone from the office had tipped her off about the raise.

He went into the kitchen, told her the good news, gave her a warm hug and a passionate kiss and then, with the kids, sat down to a wonderful, favorite meal. Sitting beside his plate was a hand-written note which read: "Congratulations, Darling!  I knew you'd get the raise. These things will tell you how much I really do love you!"

The family all chattered and enjoyed the meal together. When she got up to bring in the dessert, a card fell from her pocket. He picked it up and read: "Darling, don't worry about not getting the raise! You deserved it anyway!

These things will tell you how much I really love you!"

What a truly thoughtful and loving gesture! We could also add that she was one sharp cookie!

## Today's Special Quote

"There is something terrible about two human beings who love each other and can find neither the means or the time to let the other know, who wait until some misfortune or disagreement extorts an affirmation of affection."

*Sigmund Freud*

*Love is kind... It always protects, always trusts,*
*always hopes.*
*(I Corinthians 13:4, 7)*

# REACHING BEYOND

Do you reach beyond to touch the sky,
    or lag behind, afraid to try?
Do you reach beyond to learn anew,
    or hesitate...the same old you?
Do you reach beyond to test your limit,
    or do you tell yourself, I'm timid?
Do you reach beyond to lead the pack,
    or do you waste time looking back?
Do you reach beyond and strive to find
    better ways to stretch your mind?
Do you reach beyond to care and share
    and help some others do and dare?
Do you reach beyond, expect the best,
    or have you given up the quest?
Do you reach beyond and claim your space,
    here and now, this time, this place?
Do you reach beyond and try to soar,
    or, sadly, play it safe once more?

*Suzy Sutton*

# CLOTHED WITH COMPASSION

**A grief-stricken, widowed, now single mother** sat in the hospital lounge in stunned silence, tears streaming down her cheeks. She had just lost her only child and now she stared blindly at the wall. The head nurse talked quietly to her. "Mrs. Norris, did you notice the little boy in the hall next to your daughter's room?"

No, Mrs. Norris had not noticed him.

"Now there is a case," the nurse said. "That little boy's mother is a young Mexican woman brought in by ambulance from a shabby one-room apartment. They came to this country only three months ago seeking a new start. She had lost her husband in an accident and had no other family in Mexico and knows nobody here. They only had each other. Every day that young boy has come and sat there in the hall from sunup to sundown in hopes that his mother would awaken and speak to him."

Mrs. Norris was listening now.

"Fifteen minutes ago the mother died. Now it is my duty to tell her child that at the age of seven he is alone in this world."

The head nurse paused, then turned to Mrs. Norris. "I don't like this part of my job...I don't suppose you would go and tell him for me, would you?"

Mrs. Norris stood up, dried her tears, went and put her arms around the boy, comforted him, cried with him and led him off to her childless home. Eventually, she was able to officially adopt him. In the harshness of this life they both became a comfort to each other!

## Facing a Bleak Tomorrow

The sorrows of this life and the burden of facing an empty tomorrow are all around us.

Each day there are people who feel they have no reason or purpose for getting out of bed and on with life.

Life stretches like a wasteland before them.

They may have experienced hurt upon hurt, until there is nothing left to feel.

How about taking the time to reach out beyond yourself and touch the life of another with kindness?

*Praise be to the God and Father of our Lord Jesus Christ, the Father of compassion and the God of all comfort, who comforts us in all our troubles, so that we can comfort those in any trouble with the comfort we ourselves have received from God.*
*(II Corinthians 1:3-4)*

# THE POINT OF VIEW

**It was my privilege some years ago** to hear Corrie ten Boom speak in Milwaukee, Wisconsin. She was introduced and received an ovation before she began. She was stooped with age just a bit, dressed very humbly in a well-worn dress. Her appearance was anything but imposing.

She began speaking in a very soft voice rich with her Dutch accent. Corrie told of her upbringing and described her family. Then she began to tell of the war-torn years of the Second World War. It was not a pretty description. She related how her family hid and helped many Jewish people escape the persecution of the Nazi regime. It was a fascinating story. Every ear was intent so as not to miss a single detail.

My wife and I were sitting about half-way back in an auditorium filled with several hundred people. I had not noticed why Miss ten Boom had her head down much of the time. At first, I thought she was looking intently at her notes. But then as I paid closer attention I discovered that as she was speaking, she was working on a piece of needlepoint.

She took us on a journey to her time spent in a concentration camp. It was a sordid tale of the cruelty of human beings to other human beings. She moved on to her moment of release... her sister had died in the camp, her parents had died in this camp. It was a moving moment as she began to wrap up her story.

Corrie explained that none of us has the privilege in life to see what is really happening or why things have to happen like they do. Then... she held up the needlepoint for us to see. It was about ten by fourteen inches or so and in a frame. She showed us the back side which was nothing but a jumble of threads and colors with no discernible pattern. She went on to explain that this is how we see our lives... a view from the bottom, a view that may make no sense. Then she turned her needlework over and showed us the finished side. The pattern and colors made a beautiful scene. All the threads came together in a purpose.

She then concluded: "This is how God views your life, from the top, and someday we will have the privilege of viewing it all from his perspective."

## Today's Quote
"God must first do something for us and in us before He can do something through us."

*Eleanor Doan*

*In all things God works for the good of those who love Him, who have been called according to His purpose.*
*(Romans 8:28)*

# WHEN THERE ARE NO ANSWERS

A mother wrote the following letter to the editors of Discovery magazine and here is what was printed:

*To the Editors:*

*You won't find enclosed a picture of Peter, age 27. He's our son and he's autistic. During some of the past 27 years I have thought of murder, murder and suicide, running, moving away. I have never considered "putting him away." I have never visited any institutions, but I have a vivid imagination. I know that a non-verbal child would be in a living hell; therefore I, in my mind, turned to all those other grisly alternatives.*

*People (psychiatrists included) have said to me, "You must be special, because you cope so well," or "Your three daughters must be so compassionate." My favorite comment comes from a doctor, "Every family should have a handicapped child. It's good for the family. It unites them."*

*We could never do the "family things" except when Peter went to camp for two months. My older children no longer live at home and no longer insist that they will care for him forever.*

*The youngest, age 12, both loves and resents him and isn't too thrilled if he's around when friends visit. There isn't any answer. Nobody said it would all be fair. He exists, he is our son, we love him. I wish he had never been born.*

*It was signed by the Mother.*

Because we live in a sinful, fallen, unfair, wicked, tough place... not all life's stories will have a happy ending. There are tragedies that defy explanations. There are situations too tough to live with... yet, there's God and with Him all things become possible!

If you find yourself in such a situation, you may not find satisfactory answers to the "why" question, but there is a God in heaven who cares deeply about you, who loves you beyond all human love. He has made that fact very clear on the pages of His Word. I suggest that you begin reading from the Old Testament prophet, Isaiah chapter sixty-one.

## Skillful Navigators

"The greater the difficulty, the more glory in surmounting it. Skillful pilots gain their reputation from storms and tempests."

*Epicurus*

*The Spirit of the Lord God is upon Me, Because the Lord has anointed Me to preach good tidings to the poor; He has sent Me to heal the brokenhearted, To proclaim liberty to the captives, And the opening of the prison to those who are bound... To comfort all who mourn.*
*(Isaiah 61:1, 2b)*

# CALLING A BLUFF

**I listened and laughed as Dr. James Dobson** of "Focus on the Family" told the following about a very obnoxious ten-year-old named Robert, who happened to be a patient of Dr. William Slonecker. Robert, it seemed, at each visit to the doctor, literally attacked the pediatric clinic and his passive mother could do little to discipline him or stop him.

During one exam, Dr. Slonecker noticed cavities in Robert's teeth. But who could he refer Robert to? A referral like Robert could mean the end of a professional friendship. Dr. Slonecker decided to send him to an older dentist who reportedly understood children. The confrontation that followed must now stand as one of the classic moments in human conflict.

Robert arrived at the dental office, prepared for battle. "Get in the chair, young man," said the dentist.

"No chance!" replied Robert.

"Son, I told you to climb on to the chair and that's what I intend for you to do," said the dentist.

Robert stared at his opponent for a moment and replied, "If you make me get in that chair, I will take off all my clothes."

The dentist calmly said, "Son, take 'em off."

The boy removed his shirt, undershirt, shoes and socks, and then looked up in defiance.

"All right, son," said Dr. Slonecker, "now get in the chair."

"You didn't hear me," sputtered Robert. "I said if you make me get on that chair, I will take off ALL my clothes."

"Son, take 'em off," replied the dentist.

Robert proceeded to remove his pants and shorts, finally standing totally naked before the dentist. "Now, son, get in the chair," said the dentist.

Robert did as he was told and sat cooperatively through the entire procedure. When finished he was instructed to step down from the chair. "Give me my clothes now," said the boy.

"I'm sorry," replied the dentist. "Tell your mother that we're going to keep your clothes tonight. She can pick them up tomorrow."

Imagine the shock as the boy entered the waiting room. The room was filled with patients as Robert and his mother walked out, down an elevator, and into the parking lot.

The next day, Robert's mother returned for the clothes and told the dentist, "You don't know how much I appreciate what happened here yesterday. You see, Robert has been blackmailing me and others about his clothes for years. Whenever we are in a public place, he makes unreasonable demands of me or others with his threat. You are the first to call his bluff and the impact on Robert has been incredible!"

## Today's Thought
Among the things which are so simple that even a child can operate them are parents!

*Chasten your son while there is hope,*
*And do not set your heart on his destruction.*
*(Proverbs 19:18)*

# UNSUNG HEROES

**Susan Loomis** isn't her real name because neighbors don't sympathize with what she's doing. But her love for the four toddlers who share her modest apartment is genuine. After more than two years of red tape and government hoops to jump through, Loomis, who is in her thirties, has established the state's first permanent residence for children with AIDS. She is a registered nurse who put herself through graduate school, gave up a high paying job in a hospital and now cares for toddlers nobody else wants. She tries to fill their days with fun and love. She is the only parent for these toddlers whose parents have died from AIDS. It's her way of providing a happy childhood for kids who will likely never grow up.

**Shirley Maynard** had been married to her second husband for only two weeks when he was jailed for mail fraud and interstate theft. Her emotions ran from shock to guilt to loneliness and there was no one to turn to for help and support. She decided to help herself and her kids. Along the way she has helped many others. She founded "V.S.P." (Very Special Persons), a support group for prisoners' families, in 1984. Today there are thousands of members across the country. This Indianapolis based group offers such services as money management and aid in dealing with prison bureaucracies. Most of all, it provides a sympathetic ear.

**Norman and Ellie Chamberlain** say, "We're not giving up!" In their fifties, this couple lives in an area of crime in southeast Seattle. Instead, of giving up, they work to improve their neighborhood. Every other Saturday, they help paint over the "visual pollution" of graffiti. They helped establish a crime-tips hot line and most importantly, they help criminals go straight. They have even taken former convicts into their home to live. Sure, they were scared... but willing to take the risk!

## Making a Difference

Yes...it seems that one or two persons can truly make a difference. One is a whole number and one can make this world a better place in which to live!

"It makes you feel good if you can help someone who's down."

*Shirley Maynard*

*But do not forget to do good and to share, for with such sacrifices God is well pleased.*
*(Hebrews 13:16)*

# OF TIME AND ETERNITY

**Think...if you were to count a trillion $1 bills,** one per second, 60 per minute, 24 hours a day, it would take 32,000 years!

A "trillion" has twelve zeros. Numbers like this are beyond my comprehension. Let's explain a "trillion" in another way, perhaps we can better understand how much it is.

According to the "Statistical Abstract" of the United States for a recent year, there are about 5.7 million households in the five states of Iowa, Oklahoma, Nebraska, Kansas and Missouri. Let's account for some population growth since then and round up that number to six million households. This is how a "trillion" dollars could be spent on six million households:

Purchase a $100,000 home for each household ($600 billion).

Purchase a $10,000 second car for each household ($60 billion). We would have spent $660 billion so far.

Then for each of 250 cities, build a $10 million library and a $10 million hospital. That adds $5 billion more for a total of $665 billion spent.

Further, for each of 500 communities, erect a $10 million school, bringing our total up to $700 billion.

With what is left you could give each of 300,000 people a million dollar bonus.

"Awesome" is the only word to describe a "trillion." Yet, our government talks in terms of trillions when it thinks of a new budget! Or worse yet, our national deficit.

Alright... how about thinking in terms of a "trillion" years. Why? Have you ever given any thought to how long eternity might be? Eternity, as we understand it to be in God's Word, is forever. A trillion years and eternity would have just begun!

## Timepiece

"My timepiece may be of service to you. I have no further occasion for it. My thoughts are fixed on eternity."
*Lord William Russell, as he was about to be be-headed*

*And this is the promise that He has promised us... eternal life.*
*(I John 2:25)*

# COUNTING YOUR BLESSINGS

**Helen was born with more birth defects** than you might think possible: only one lung, one kidney, mis-shapened nose and ears, a cleft palate so deep that speech was incredibly difficult, almost totally deaf and destined to become blind.

She was cruelly teased by other children and depressed by parental neglect. Helen became so desperate about her situation that she asked a friend to take her to church. There she learned to pray and to place her trust and faith in God whose loving arms would hold her safe in spite of everything. Her church friends found doctors to perform surgeries on her eyes and ears but the operations failed. They helped her enroll in a school for the blind to prepare for a life of total darkness.

Years passed and communication steadily became more difficult for Helen. One Christmas Eve, at the midnight service back in Helen's friendly home church, the pastor was offering Communion. A young woman approached the table... there was a pause as she did not seem to hear the invitation to accept the elements of the bread and wine.

Then, with a gasp of astonishment, the minister recognized Helen, noticed her white cane and understood why she did not see the Communion emblems presented to her. Also he knew why she had not heard his voice in offering them. Deeply moved, he leaned forward to kiss her and a tear fell on her cheek. But it was not Helen's tear... you see, she was also born without tear ducts. Even the comfort of having a good cry had been denied her because of her physical problems.

The pastor indicated to Helen that she should stay behind after the rest of the Christmas crowd had left so she could visit with him in his office. Later, in the office, struggling to express her emotions through her repaired cleft palate, Helen's words tumbled out. She told her pastor that although what little vision she'd had was now gone, her faith in God was stronger than ever. She expressed her love for God at this Christmas season. She told about her schooling and about the struggles in life that she faced and hopefully, a bit about her future. She said that she was the most fortunate one in her class for the blind. In her halting words she said, "I'm so blessed to have had what I had, because I'm the only one in the class who remembers what it was like to be able to see!"

## Gratitude

"Gratitude is born in hearts that take time to count up past mercies."

*Charles E. Jefferson*

*It is good to give thanks to the LORD,*
*And to sing praises to Your name, O Most High;*
*To declare Your loving kindness in the morning,*
*And your faithfulness every night...*
*(Psalm 92:1-2)*

# THE RIGHT ATTITUDE

**Kelley Roswell, at age eleven,** was a Little League softball player. She played shortstop and pitcher for the Grand Mesa Major girls all-stars. She loved softball. She could hardly wait for springtime to roll around so she could get back on the field to play. That's not all... Kelley was an outstanding student in school and refused to settle for anything less than an "A" in any of her classes.

Kelley was young and normally people this young don't deserve the label of "hero," but in my estimation she is very deserving. I don't think she could be considered just an ordinary girl... she had one major problem in life: Kelley Roswell, age eleven, had leukemia!

Since it was diagnosed in March of 1988, she had been in a life-and-death battle with the disease. On March 14, her diagnoses was confirmed: she had "ALL," otherwise known as "Acute Lumphocytic Leukemia" (commonly known as childhood leukemia). As a result, she traveled to Denver, Colorado and spent weeks in the Children's Hospital in an earnest battle for her life. Her first stay lasted about a month in which chemotherapy was begun. This was followed by a daily medication of pills. She had to return to Denver from Grand Junction, Colorado every week for a time. This was reduced to a return trip every six weeks. The four-hour trips, injections, transfusions and pills had all been taken in stride by Kelley, without complaint. Normally, chemotherapy has the side effects of vomiting and nausea but according to her father, Steve, she had no major problems. She never did get sick from the treatments.

Her mother, Joanne said, "As a mother, I could be weepy, but Kelley hasn't allowed that. God gave us Kelley and we've learned that the time we have with her is special. We feel humbled from all the support we've received. God's had His hand on Kelley. God gives us children as gifts and they belong to Him. We get them for only a certain amount of time."

The Roswells are a committed church family. They have acknowledged that prayers and other kinds of support have been sources of strength and help as offered from their church and community.

Even leukemia didn't slow Kelley in playing her beloved softball. During the summer of 1988, she didn't just show up, she was a real star, pitching and hitting her team to a second place finish! Anyway you look at it, Kelley was a real winner! And, oh yes, Kelley did beat leukemia, too! She's disease free today.

## Believe

"I can believe that one day every bruise and every leukemia cell and every embarrassment and every hurt will be set right, and all those grim moments of hoping against hope will be rewarded."

*Phillip Yancey*

*And He said to me, "My grace is sufficient for you, for My strength is made perfect in weakness." Therefore most gladly I will rather boast in my infirmities, that the power of Christ may rest upon me. (II Corinthians 12:9)*

# OUT OF THE MOUTHS OF BABES

**Nancy Biedebach shared this event from her life.** It was winter and Nancy was walking along the beach at Emerald Bay in Laguna, California. The beach was nearly deserted. She felt the need to be alone with God in prayer and truly cry out to Him for comfort, direction and help. She was struggling with family concerns along with some deep personal needs. The day happened to be clear but cold and the ocean was beautiful. She felt very much aware of God's world...and His presence surrounding her. Yet, she needed God to speak to the immediate problems she, as a mother, faced.

Suddenly she was aware of God's communicating in her mind the instruction: "Write it down in the sand." She looked around and found a small stick and wrote these four words in the damp sand, one under the other:

*Jesus*
*Please*
*Help*
*Me*

As she finished the last word, a small shadow fell over her shoulder where she knelt. A very young boy, perhaps about seven, was standing there. He took the stick from her hand without comment. At first Nancy was sorry that anyone had seen what she had written. She felt it had been a very private expression and cry to God.

But the little boy smiled at her and made the sign of the cross in the sand right over the name of Jesus and said "I am a Christian." At this, he turned back to two other children who were with him and the three of them walked on down the beach without another word.

God had simply met her with the message of the cross through a little child. God touched her with the profound truth, once more.

## Today's Quote

"Every child comes with the message that God is not yet discouraged with humankind."

*Rabindrinath Tagore*

*Jesus... said to them,*
*"Let the little children come to Me, and do not forbid them;*
*for of such is the kingdom of God.*
*Assuredly, I say to you, whoever does not receive the kingdom of*
*God as a little child will by no means enter it."*
*And He took them up in His arms,*
*laid His hands on them, and blessed them."*
*(Mark 10:14-16)*

# A WHODUNIT

**Two men, an army major general and his young first lieutenant,** were traveling from one military base to another in Europe when they were forced to travel with civilians aboard a passenger train. They found their compartment, where two people were already seated: a very attractive young lady and obviously her mother. For most of the trip they conversed freely. It was turning out to be a most enjoyable trip for all four of them.

Then the train entered a long dark tunnel; besides no lights being on in the tunnel, there were none in the compartment either. Once inside the tunnel, the four passengers heard two distinct sounds: the first was the loud smooch of a kiss, the second was the sharp sound of a hard slap! Here is each person's interpretation of what was just heard.

The young lady is pleased to think that the handsome young lieutenant got up the courage to try to kiss her. But she is somewhat disappointed in that he had mistakenly kissed her mother, who apparently had slapped him for his trouble.

The major general is amused with his lieutenant because of his romantic enterprise, but chagrined at the young woman because of the hard slapping of him instead of his lieutenant.

The mother is also taken aback to think that the young officer would have the gall to kiss her daughter, but she is also proud of her daughter for slapping him in return.

But of all the passengers in this car, only one really knows what happened in the darkened tunnel... and he is not about to tell! The young lieutenant is having a very tough time holding back the laughter as he observes the expressions on the other three faces and the red slap mark on the general's face. This handsome, young, enterprising lieutenant found the perfect opportunity to slap his superior officer, hard... after kissing the back of his own hand!

## Creativity

Where there's a will, there is also a way!
Why not consider applying that concept to whatever life situation you might find yourself facing?
There is a way! There is an answer! There is a resolution!
And... there is a creative God for you to call upon in your need!

*If any of you lacks wisdom, let her ask of God,*
*who gives to all liberally and without reproach,*
*and it will be given to her.*
*(James 1:5)*

# FIFTY IS NIFTY... OR IS IT?

**On my fiftieth birthday,** my older daughter gave me a pin that said: "50 is Nifty." I wore it to work that day and what fun it was! All day, people kept saying things to me like, "Anita, you don't look fifty," or "Why, Anita, you can't be fifty," and "We know you can't be fifty."

It was wonderful. Now, I knew they were lying and they knew I knew, but isn't that what friends and coworkers do? To encourage you when you need it, in times of emergency, like divorce, death and turning 50.

You know how it is with such flattery, though. You hear it often enough and you begin to think its true. By the end of the day I felt fabulous. I fairly floated home from work. In fact, on the way home, I thought: "I might think about dumping my husband... after all, the geezer was fifty-one, way too old for a young-looking gal like me."

Arriving home, I had just shut the front door when the doorbell rang. It was a young girl from the florist shop, bringing birthday flowers from a friend. They were lovely. I stood there holding the flowers and admiring them, and the delivery girl stood there, waiting for a tip.

She noticed the pin on my jacket and said, "Oh, fifty, eh?"

"Yes," I answered, and waited. I could stand one last compliment before my birthday ended.

"Fifty," she repeated. "That's great! Birthday or anniversary?"

*Anita Cheek Milner, Chocolate for a Woman's Soul, Fireside, New York, NY, 1997, adapted*

One day as I was picking
 the toys off the floor,
I noticed a small hand print
 on the wall beside the door.
I knew that it was something
 that I'd seen most every day,
but this time when I saw it there,
 I wanted it to stay.
Then tears welled up inside my eyes,
 I knew it wouldn't last,
for every mother knows
 her children grow up way too fast.
Just then I put my chores aside
 and held my children tight.
I sang to them sweet lullabies
 and rocked into the night.
Sometimes we take for granted,
 all those things that seem so small.
Like one of God's great treasures…
 A small hand print on the wall.

*Source is unknown*

"Attention is like a daily bouquet of love."
*Bob Keeshan, otherwise known as "Captain Kangaroo"*

*Behold, children are a heritage from the Lord,*
*The fruit of the womb is a reward.*
*Like arrows in the hand of a warrior,*
*So are the children of one's youth.*
*(Psalm 127:3-4)*

# INSTRUCTIONS FOR LIFE FROM 40 MOMS

1. *Give people more than they expect and do it cheerfully.*
2. *Memorize your favorite poem.*
3. *Don't believe all you hear, spend all you have or sleep all you want.*
4. *When you say, "I love you," mean it.*
5. *When you say, "I'm sorry," look the person in the eye.*
6. *Be engaged at least twelve months before you get married.*
7. *Believe in love at first sight.*
8. *Never laugh at anyone's dreams, including those of your own kids.*
9. *Love deeply and passionately. You might get hurt but it's the only way to live life completely.*
10. *In disagreements, fight fairly. No name calling.*
11. *Don't judge other people by their relatives.*
12. *Talk slowly but think quickly.*
13. *When someone asks you a question you don't want to answer, smile and ask, "Why do you want to know?"*
14. *Remember that great love and great achievement involve great risk.*
15. *Say "God bless you" when you hear someone sneeze.*
16. *When you lose… don't lose the lesson learned.*
17. *Remember the three Rs: Respect for self; Respect for others; Responsibility for all your actions.*
18. *Don't let a little dispute injure a great friendship.*
19. *When you realize you've made a mistake, take immediate steps to correct it.*
20. *Smile when picking up the phone. The caller will hear it in your voice.*
21. *Marry a man you love to talk to. As you get older, his conversational skills will be as important as any other.*

22. *Spend some time alone.*
23. *Open your arms to change, but don't let go of your values.*
24. *Remember that silence is sometimes the best answer.*
25. *Read more books and watch a whole lot less TV.*
26. *Live a good, honorable life. Then when you get older and think back, you'll get to enjoy it a second time.*
27. *Trust in God and other people but lock your car and your house.*
28. *A loving atmosphere in your home is so important. Do all you can to create a tranquil, harmonious home.*
29. *In disagreements with loved ones, deal with the current situation. Don't bring up the past.*
30. *Read between the lines...always.*
31. *Share your knowledge and wisdom. It's a way to achieve immortality.*
32. *Be gentle with the earth; after all, God created it.*
33. *Pray. There's immeasurable power in it.*
34. *Never interrupt when you are being flattered. Just say a simple "Thank you."*
35. *Mind your own business.*
36. *Don't trust a man who doesn't close his eyes when you kiss.*
37. *Once a year, go some place you've never been before.*
38. *If you make a lot of money, put it to use helping others while you are living. That is wealth's greatest satisfaction.*
39. *Remember that not getting what you want is sometimes a stroke of very good fortune.*
40. *Learn the rules, then break some. Act outside the box sometimes.*

# SHOWING US THE WAY

**When Atlanta Hawks center Theo Ratliff** was growing up, his mother, Camillia, provided the everyday lesson on perseverance. Daily, after the hour-long commute from her factory job to home in Demopolis, a small rural town in Alabama, she took her books and studied late into the night working on a college degree.

"She was an influence by showing us the way, not just telling us," says Theo who has two brothers, Thad and Tim. "Getting her degree was something she was dedicated to doing. That's the type of lesson she gave: If you want it enough, you can get it done no matter what."

Theo kept that lesson in mind as he relentlessly practiced his basketball growing up. The example of mom helped him to become an NBA (National Basketball Association) All-Star, a good father and a responsible, generous citizen.

To raise her three sons, Camillia held down as many as four jobs at once. Obviously the family didn't have much but their focus was never on the material things of life… rather it was centered on the wealth of a loving family. Camillia said, "We were rich. Sometimes you wish for bigger, better, more. But sometimes coming up the rough side of the mountain isn't so bad."

The boys took part in every activity they could fit into a busy growing-up life… Key Club, honor society, museum visits, plays, church functions and sports. They did it all and kept up good grades, too. "Without that type of influence from within their families, a lot of our friends went astray," Theo says.

He worked hard at his hoops… sometimes angering mother's wrath by skipping the chores posted on the refrigerator door. "She always would say, 'Whatever it is you choose to do in life, try to be the best at it,'" he says. "That's how I've approached my game and being a parent."

Because of his life principles, learned from mom, he was awarded a scholarship to Wyoming University. He almost quit basketball after his second year but Camillia told him, "Winners never quit, and quitters never win." That was the turning point...from that moment on, Theo excelled. Detroit selected him in the first round of the 1995 NBA draft.

The rest is history... Theo is an All-Star; he and his wife, Kristina, have two daughters; he's involved in community events which give back; Camillia has her college degree and manages elder-care programs in ten Alabama counties! Yes, mother knows best!

*Brad Young, Hershey's Presents Parents & Kids,*
*Advertising Feature, 2001 Time, Inc. Condensed and adapted*

## Today's Quote

"Camillia might not have taught Theo anything about jump shots or blocked shots. But what he learned from her has as much to do with his success as anything a coach ever said."

*Brad Young*

*Therefore we also, since we are surrounded by so great a cloud of witnesses, let us lay aside every weight, and the sin which so easily ensnares us, and let us run with endurance the race that is set before us, looking unto Jesus, the author and finisher of our faith... (Hebrews 12:1-2a)*

# A LITTLE JOG FOR YOUR HEART HEALTH

**Why do they come to see Ben Comen run?** Why come to see a kid finish the 3.1 mile cross-country run in more than 51 minutes when the winner crosses the finish line in about 16 minutes? Why do they cry when they watch him run? Why do teammates and visiting teams go back on the course to run the final ten minutes of every race with him? Why do they hug this teen when he has never won a race? WHY?

You see Ben has a huge heart, he also has cerebral palsy, but it didn't affect his mind... he's an A and B student. This disease grabs muscles and contorts his body and leaves him off balance. Why does he compete for the Hanna High cross-country team in Anderson, South Carolina? Why?

"Because I feel like I've been put here to set an example," said Ben, age 16. "Anybody can find something they can do... and do it well. I like to show people that you can either stop trying or you can pick yourself up and keep going. It's just more fun to keep going."

Ben has two healthy brothers who run like rabbits for Hanna High. He runs like a man swatting bees. Imagine never beating anybody. Imagine falling hard... his brain doesn't send signals fast enough for his arms to cushion his fall, so often, he smacks his head, face or shoulders. Often, his parents can't watch.

"I've been coaching cross-country for 31 years," says Hanna's Chuck Parker, "and I've never met anyone with the drive that Ben has. I don't think there's an inch of that kid I haven't had to bandage up." But never before he finishes the race... he always finishes, bloody and bruised but never beaten! He hasn't quit a single race!

In a recent race, Ben is coming in with his army, his friends, his teammates, his face is beet red, laborious, eating up the course an inch at a time, arms flailing... he's about ten yards from the finish line and he falls smack on his face, again! A gasp goes up from the parents… silence from the other kids. Nobody helps him…because he refuses help. He goes through a fifteen-second process of getting his bloodied knees under him, regains his wobbling balance… and into forward motion… he's not embarrassed, he's just mad he fell… and across the finish line!

You'd have thought he'd won the Boston Marathon! "Words can't describe that moment," says his mom. "I saw grown men just stand there and cry." Yes, Ben can get to you.

*Thanks to Rick Reilly*

How did he get this determination, this drive? From the start he was this determined kid… but others tell us it comes from the support of his family, his parents, his siblings, his support system!

## Feeling a Bit Down?

"Do you need a special dose of humanity? Get yourself to Hanna. And while you're there, go out and join Ben's friends. You'll be amazed what a little jog can do for your heart!"

*Rick Reilly*

*We have this treasure in earthen vessels, that the excellence of the power may be of God and not of us.*
*We are hard pressed on every side, yet not crushed…*
*(II Corinthians 4:7-9)*

# IN TRIBUTE TO THE AMERICAN SPIRIT

**Perhaps you have seen or purchased one of her unique art pieces.**
Cindy Shamp started painting in 1989 out of the need to do something for
herself. Choosing to be a stay-at-home mom, Cindy found that she could be
available to her two daughters and still paint things to sell at small shows.

"I had been painting mostly on wood that my husband cut out for me,"
said Shamp. "My husband's military career took him off to war and I found
myself with nothing to paint on. That's when I developed a way to paint on
metal."

Having known since she was a little girl that she could draw, she took
advantage of the paint brush collection given to her by her husband's grandmother and discovered she loved to paint. "The designs that I came up with
mostly were related to the flag whether it was an Uncle Sam Santa or an
Angel with flag wings. This is what really got me started and motivated about
painting. I would design an ornament, cut it out myself and then paint it.
I painted my first design on watercolor paper with acrylic paints in 1998."

She credits her marriage to a military man for influencing her views on life.
This is a decision that he doesn't take lightly, which has affected not only
Shamp but others who see her art works. She says, "After going through
several wars I have faced life and the death of people I have actually known.
The only way I have survived all these situations is through my faith in God.
Inspiring words combined with the Americana touch is how I see my paint-
ings evolving through the years."

## Today's Quote

"I love to paint what makes me feel peaceful, with a subdued message.

I would like everyone to be thankful for the country they live in and take pride in their heritage.

I like the look of days gone by... simpler times... peacefulness, especially since the events of September 11."

*Cindy Shamp, artist*

*One thing I have desired of the LORD,*
*That I will seek:*
*That I may dwell in the house of the LORD*
*All the days of my life,*
*To behold the beauty of the LORD.*
*(Psalm 27:4)*

# THE VIRTUES OF WOMEN AND MEN

## WOMEN:

Women have strengths that amaze men. They carry children, they carry hardships, carry burdens, but they also hold happiness, love and joy. They smile when they want to scream. They sing when they want to cry. They cry when they are happy and laugh when they are nervous. Women wait by the phone for a "safe-at-home-call" from a friend after a snowy drive home. Women have special qualities about them. They volunteer for good causes. They are pink ladies in hospitals, they bring food to shut-ins. They are child care workers, executives, attorneys, stay-at-home moms, biker babes and your neighbors. They fight for what they believe in. They stand up for injustice. They are in the front row at PTA meetings. They walk and talk the extra mile to get their children in the right schools and for getting their family the right health care. They stick a love note in their spouse's lunch box. They do without new shoes so their children can have them. They go to the doctor with a frightened friend. They love unconditionally. Women are honest, loyal and forgiving. They are smart, knowing that knowledge is power. But they still know how to use their softer side to make a point. Women want to be the best for their family, their friends and themselves. They cry when their children excel and cheer when their friends get awards. They are happy when they hear about a birth or a new marriage. Their hearts break when a friend dies. They have sorrow at the loss of a family member, yet they are strong when they think there is no strength left. Women drive, fly, walk, run or e-mail you to show how much they care about you. The heart of a woman is what makes the world spin! Women do more than just give birth. They bring joy and hope. They give compassion and ideals. They give moral support to their family and friends. They make sure the family is part of a good church. They give encouragement to discouraged family and friends. AND all they want back is a hug, a smile and for you to do the same to people you come in contact with. YES!

## MEN:
Well... that's for another chapter and book. But in the meantime men are good at lifting heavy stuff and killing bugs.

## Inner Peace Attained

"To attain inner peace you must actually give your life, not just your possessions. When you at last give your life... bringing into alignment your beliefs and the way you live... then, and only then can you begin to find inner peace."

*Peace Pilgrim*

*"Many daughters have done well, But you excel them all.*
*Charm is deceitful and beauty is passing,*
*But a woman who fears the LORD, she shall be praised.*
*Give her of the fruit of her hands,*
*And let her own works praise her in the gates."*
*(Proverbs 31:29-31)*

*Dear Heavenly Father:*

*Make me a better parent. Help me to understand my children, to listen patiently to what they have to say and to answer all their questions kindly. Keep me from interrupting them, talking back to them and contradicting them. Make me as courteous to them as I would have them be to me. Give me the courage to confess my sins against my children and ask them forgiveness, when I know I have done wrong.*

*Forbid that I should laugh at their mistakes or resort to shame and ridicule as punishment. Let me not tempt a child to lie or steal. So guide me hour by hour and day by day that I may demonstrate by all I say and do that honesty produces happiness.*

*Reduce, I pray, the meanness in me. May I cease to nag and when I am out of sorts, Oh Lord, to hold my tongue. Give me a ready word for honest praise.*

*Allow me not to rob them of the opportunity to grow up into responsible human beings, the desire to wait on themselves, to think, to choose and to make their own decisions.*

*Make me fair and just and loving. Help me to be considerate and compassionate and a companion to my children... to the point that they will have genuine esteem for me. Fit me to be loved and imitated by my children. Oh, God, please give me calm and poise and self-control in all of my life situations. Help me to be like your Son in attitude and love so that my children will also be like your Son in life choices and actions.*

***AMEN***